I WANTED TO BE IN LOVE

Poems by
Erik Rivas

Erik Rivas
Brooklyn, New York

Copyright © 2019 Erik Rivas. All rights reserved. No part of this publication may be reproduced, stored in or introduced into a retrieval system, or transmitted, in any form or by any means (electronic, mechanical, photocopying, recording or otherwise), without the prior written permission of the copyright owner.

The scanning, uploading, and distribution of this book via the Internet or any other means without the permission of the publisher are illegal and punishable by law. Please purchase only authorized electronic editions and do not participate in or encourage electronic piracy of copyrighted materials. Your support of the author's rights is appreciated.

Limits of Liability ~ Disclaimer

The author and publisher shall not be liable for your misuse of this material. This book is strictly for expressive purposes. The author and publisher shall have neither liability nor responsibility to anyone concerning any loss or damage caused, or alleged to be caused, directly or indirectly by the information contained in this book.

Cover Design: Okomota
Editing-Interior Layout: The Self-Publishing Maven
Formatting: Chris P

ISBN: 978-1-7329608-0-0

Printed in the United States of America

TABLE OF CONTENTS

SUMMER 2015............4

FALL 2015............14

WINTER 2015/2016............27

SPRING 2016............52

SUMMER 2016............92

FALL 2016............109

WINTER 2016/17............135

SPRING 2017............162

Summer 2015

Be My DJ

I wish I could listen to
What you're listening to
I wish you could be my DJ
Just give me one of your headphones
And you can pick which songs to play

You stroll in like a golden omen
From me you sit across
In your music you were lost
I want to know the songs you're playing
I want to know what keeps you swaying
I feel a strong connection
Can't stop looking in your direction
I know we're strangers
And you might not want to talk to me
But I don't see nothing wrong
With you showing me your favorite songs

I wish I could listen to

What you're listening to

I wish you could be my DJ

Just give me one of your headphones

And you can pick which songs to play

Summer Tease

I met you, just last year
I was hoping, you'd be back here
We had a nice cool conversation
Our laughter was a smooth flirtation
I was feelin' you from the beginning
Your lips were stunningly grinning
But then I stepped away for a minute
I came back to your seat
But you weren't in it
I didn't get your name
I didn't get your number
All I got was a tease in the Summer
Summer Tease
Sort of like a summer breeze
Comes and goes
As it please
On the hottest day
She'll make you freeze
With such ease
And then she leaves

Unfogotten Love

It ended on a bad note

A violin's broken string

A pain that crushes your chest within

It stings to think what could have been

And what was

But I believe

We gave it all we could

We'll save what was good

We had memories that drift through the wind

We see them lift and descend again and again

Midnight Kiss

Lingerie on the floor

Covers crammed to the foot of the bed

Moonlight glistening off your curves

Kissing the blue gray

Caressing the night shade

The evening was made for this

Intoxicated from the midnight mist

Inhale every kiss

Aggressive movements

Slowing down only to catch our breaths

Then back at it again

Soothing sessions

Smooth but powerful

A rhythm with heavy drums

A melody of moans

In a zone we can't dethrone

Until we both…

A Future With You

Strolling through the greens of the land

Holding on to the squeeze of your hand

Let's build our dream home

Let's plant a garden

I'm starving for a reason to celebrate

I'm carving your name on a wooden gate

I want to toast to you

I'll give the most to you

Withered

Can such a beautiful thing just turn to dust

Can a kingdom just lose its reign

It seems we've lost the trust

Our dreams have turned to shame

Spontaneous

Can I take you for a ride

Let's not plan a thing

Just go outside

See what surprises life can bring

I know you like to be organized

You stick to a strict schedule

I'll show you how to improvise

How to stay away from the dull

The Actress

I walked passed you

I instantly got hit with your beauty

I had to turn back

Your eyes were down

But I recognized your bone structure

And the softness around it

You're that actress I saw on TV

You looked nice on the screen

But you were flawless in person

I stared from a distance

I tried to develop the bravery

But didn't have the nerve to speak to you

I felt a pressure in my chest

A battle with my lungs

Too much time passed

Then finally I decided to let some words flow

But that's when you had to go

And the train doors closed

Fall 2015

A Lost Angel

I thought I had destiny in my grasp

We joked and laughed

We shared something special

But I guess a moment is all we had

I really thought this could have been it

You seemed so perfect

My dream girl

My goddess

My angel

I'll never know why

What did I do wrong?

What did I say?

To make my angel fly away

I was making plans

Thinking of all the things we can do

All the places we can go

But now I realize that my thoughts were a waste

It's written all over my frustrated face

You were my dream girl

My goddess

My angel

What did I do wrong?

What did I say?

To make my angel fly away

Too Addictive

Why can't I stay away?

I told myself I want to be alone

I don't need nobody

But all it takes

Is a couple of shakes

A swing of the hips

A smile in the street

And I'm weak

The curves, the words, the essence

It's a blessing and a curse

Can't stop thinking about her

Can't stop looking at her

So intoxicated, inebriated, elevated

I can't take it

She got me in her trap

Latched to her lap

Closure

I hope you're happy

I hope you're okay

You deserve security

You deserve a way

To portray all your beauty

Your grin penetrates my skin

Your laugh warms everything within

I can tell you're in a good place

I'm not even jealous

I'm glad that you've found peace

I notice the power of the love

You've been given

I'll just enjoy your essence from a distance

Not Sure

It sucks now that it's over

So many memories, so many gifts

Now they're all in the abyss

Did I want out of this place?

Or did I just want space?

Sometimes you want to jump off the edge

Sometimes you just need to look down

Just Wondering

I can't help but wonder

What it would be like

If you weren't taken

Would we click

Would the chemistry be like electricity

Or would we be better off as just friends

I would never cross that boundary

I will respect your relationship

I can control my actions

But I can't control my thoughts

So they run wild

Running through all types of scenarios

Who's It Going To Be?

Love is hovering me

But when will it truly cover me

There's faces I like

And bodies I desire

Who will be the one

Is it the lady on the bus

Staring out the dirty window

Is it the woman I haven't heard from in a while

Now she's around and lives within a mile

Will it be the friend of mine

Who teases all the time

Will it be someone so close to me

That we'll mend so tremendously

Is it the lady at the bar

She wants to take more shots of Patrón

But all her friends want to go home

High Standards

What if your smile is enough
Cause the others don't measure up
We can't be together, that much is true
But I still compare all of them to you

Can't fall in love
Can't even give others a chance
Can't let go
Can't say yes

One day I will find someone better than you
One day I will find someone brand new
But until that day comes I'll pretend to…

Wrong

I've been chasing you for so long

But I had it all wrong

I always had you

I was just trying too hard

I've been crushing on you for so long

But I had it all wrong

I was always in love

I just had up my guard

So now we're ready

Ready to be what we're supposed to be

Now I can feel, without being afraid

Now I can heal, with your love as my aid

Can I?

Can I see you this evening?

Can I feel what I've been dreaming?

I need to feel your skin

I need to soak it all in

I need your energy

I love your sympathy

The way you look at me

Your magic

I just gotta have it

Like raindrops falling on thirsting leaves

Like hilltops calling the searching breeze

No Resolution

We left pretty upset

Nothing much accomplished yet

All we do is argue

Because we sense the end is near

I don't want to walk away

But maybe I already have

Nothing feels pure anymore

Everything is old and repetitive

We have no more to give

It's sad but it's the truth

It's a shame but it's the only way

I see your tears

I feel your pain

It's not fair

But we have to go there

You Deserve To Soar

I miss the way you would stare

Little things to show that you care

The way you would rub my head

Build up my ego with the things you said

Maybe you were too precious to keep inside

So go fly in the endless sky

With your relentless drive

Winter 2015/16

Tu Cuerpo

I need your body enveloping mine

I need the passion of your grind

I need to hear you breathe in ecstasy

While I thrust in and out of reality

I need you now more than ever

Will you do me the pleasure?

A Sketch

I hear the rain dripping

I feel my chance slipping

I know it's far fetched

But I wish I could sketch

A portrait of a blue ocean and blue sky

With a boat a float, where two lovers lie

Not a care in the air

And so much time to spare

You Know It

Don't you wish that you could kiss these lips

I bet you're craving the love making

You can tell we would hit it off

Gonna make you bite your bottom lip off

It's getting so hot but I don't wanna cool off

Keep sweating until I tear your roof off

Make The Night Cry

We make the night cry

We make the night cry

The thunder pounds around us

The water can drown us

The stars are dimming in the sky

The cars are swimming outside

All this commotion is in rhythm with our emotions

The passion that's crashing within

Causing the entire atmosphere to perspire

Ending droughts and forest fires

No longer will the land be dry

Because…

We make the night cry

We make the night cry

Winter Heat

It's a winter night in the city

So brick. It might even snow

But you still want to see me

I'm getting ready to go

One last look in the mirror

Grab my coat, head outside

The wind hits like a hammer

Take the train ride

I'm meeting you at Rockefeller

Can't wait to kiss your warm lips

Your skin will feel like a furnace

Who Knows?

Maybe destiny put us here

Maybe misery needs company

Maybe the universe is weird

Maybe it's our astrology

Maybe luck has nothing to do with it

Maybe we deserve more credit

We chose to be with each other

Were not measly star-crossed lovers

Travel Guide

Are you woman enough to ask?

Are you up for the task?

I don't mind to be given direction

As long as it leads to satisfaction

If you want to be my guide

I'll follow you for the whole ride

How do you want to be touched?

Soft or rough?

Where do you want to be kissed?

On your neck or your lips?

How and where, I don't care

I'm down for whatever, I swear

In the mood, I'm so damn excited

But I'll keep it under control with some guidance

See a man can be animalistic and just want to rush and pound

But with instructions he can slow it down

Fantasizing

I lose track of time when you cross my mind

Endless fantasies formulate

Keep me up so late

No dream can be better than my own desires

I know exactly how to create the perfect love story

And it always ends with you falling for me

There's no other way

No other way this tale should end

If I'm going to pretend

I'm going to imagine a summer day

With you and I at the beach's edge

So many false alarms

So many disappointments

But something about you

Gives me hope

Something about you

Brings back the goosebumps

Games

I think you know what's up

We've been playing too much

Enough is enough

Let's do more than flirt

Some lovin' won't hurt

I know you're just as curious

So let's start this monogamous genesis

Things Done Changed

We used to be so tight

I had your back, and you had mine

We shined but in time, things got dim

You said some stuff

I thought it was a bluff

But it ended up being the truth

You cracked the ceiling and blew the roof

You destroyed the love I had for you

Instead of trying to repair it

I just let it break down

I was too exhausted to afford this

Still Hoping

Walking in the scorching desert

Looking for a mermaid

Just doesn't make much sense

But I have dreams and so do you

I believe that love can be anywhere

My journey might be long and tiresome

Then so be it

I'll wait it out, if it means a happy ending

If it means my energy ascending

I'll take my time, if it's worth it

This life I live, I will never curse it

I find blessings in the most dire of situations

I've been beaten down

But I have patience

I've fallen so many times

But I continue to make it

Sorceress

Look at her

She'll make you fall in love in a blur

You'll spend the most

Money, time, and energy

She's a true beauty

From head to toe

You'll follow her motto

She'll convert you

To her purple circle

Transform you

Just to warn you

If you want a chance

You need to learn her dance

Take lessons on how to woo her

You thought you knew her

But you have no idea

This woman has no fear

She'll swim with the sharks

She'll wrestle with a bear

Break the ballers' hearts

Take all that's there

She changes men

Makes them fight for attention

In the night you'll question

If she's a nightmare or a blessing

Are you close?

Or far as hell?

With her you can never tell

Dumbfounded

Empty handed

Empty hearted

So empty since we parted

It will get better I know

But for now

It's such a deep sorrow

Walking in the street

I looked so lost

I have to pause

And figure out where I'm going

Things are confusing

We did everything together

So even the small things are tough

I have the memories

But that's not enough

It's like a kiss from the cursed

Feels good at first

Then makes things worse

Fear

I'm looking forward to
Though I barely I know you
I'm getting nervous
Don't want to mess this up
But knowing me, I might do it on purpose
I would ruin things
Before it even bloomed
Cut it off too soon
Such a pessimistic view
But I think it's true
Thinking realistically
Can mean standing still
Too afraid to travel

Book Borrow

I know it might sound insane

But I fell in love on a train

Saw a goddess walk in

Sit down and pull out a book

I couldn't help but look

I recognized the title

So I asked her if she thought it was good

She said if I get a chance to read it, I should

It tells the stories of two lovers

That met on a mountaintop

Under the rain drops

They didn't even speak

They just smiled and stared

Their dreams had brought them there

Voices coming from somewhere

Telling them to go to the mountain

Where the clouds make a fountain

I told her that the book sounds very interesting

Can I borrow it please?

She laughed and asked how I would return it

I replied that I would like to meet her

Where the land reaches for the sky's hand

Where the rain caresses the two guests

Should Have

I was hoping you still looked at me like you used to

But it seems that you moved on

You've grown so much

Now I'm the one with the crush

So many men are infatuated

You've made it

You have such a long list

I think I'm on the bottom now

But back in the day

I know you were crazy about me

And now it's my turn to live in jealousy

Sunrise To Sundown

The sun shows its face

The birds sing their song

I'm in a haste

The day is just not long enough

So I cherish every second

I run to find you

Do you want to play a game?

Do you want to walk by the lake?

Just please spend the day with me

And when the moon comes

Can we close our eyes together

Try

I remember the old days

We used to chill all the time

We got close, but not enough I suppose

We stayed connected through the years

But now I think I'm ready to face my fears

We should be more than friends

We should try this again

I'll Show Her

She's always busy

Has no time for me

I know I should let go

But the possibilities

And the fantasies

Keep me from trying

She probably doesn't even think about me

She's fine being without me

But all I want is one more night

One chance to show her I'm Mr Right

She will be so surprised

She doesn't know how good I am

Strangers

I apologize, I thought I saw something in your eyes

But still I don't want to approach if I'm not sure

Your beauty I adore

And I want to know more

I wonder if I can make you smile

If I spoke to you

Would you be engaged or enraged

Want To

Want to run my hands all over them curves

Want to squeeze the thickness of your sexiness

Want to tease the curiosity of your senses

Want to lick your skin outside and in

Want to make you moan louder than the morning waves

Want to take you to the ecstasy that your body craves

Want to taste all your passion as you scream

Want to lace you with my marble glass streams

Werewolves

Where do you think you're going?

I'm not done

Not even close

You have so much more to give

This is how I live

Don't stop until you have none left

You can take a break

But nobody's leaving anytime soon

I want you moaning to the moon

Until the sunrise burns our eyes

All night and early morning

We'll be glowing

Keep on going

Cause I have an appetite

For your mighty bite

Spring 2016

Hooked

I wish I could lie with you
Time would just fly with you
Want to spend the night with you
Spend my life with you
I just might with you

The Beginning

I have to daydream about you

Because I can't sleep without you

Got me up all night, so damn restless

Wishing your lips I could kiss

Your body I could caress

But instead it's just me in this bed

Begging the sky to send you a message

That the stars have our blessing

I miss you and barely know you

But I know if I hold you

You can learn so much from my touch

Our hearts will beat together

Cause we need each other

Double Broke

Looking back was it all worth it

Watching others get it

Don't I deserve it

I think I earned it

But I guess not

I gave it my best shot

Should I just pack it in

Start relaxing

In a life of slight satisfaction

With a wife that's lacking

Just settle for something mediocre

Following my dreams is over

Cause it hurt so hard

To work so hard

And to come home with nothing

Nothing in my pocket

Nothing in my heart locket

Running Late

Was it fate that made me run late

Was it destiny that gave me the opportunity

Was there an unseen force that put us on course

Was there a spell that made us gel

Either way I'm happy there was an empty seat

I'm happy we got a chance to meet

I was staring at you for awhile

Thinking of a way to make you smile

Waiting for the perfect opportunity

I didn't want this moment to slip away

Not today

I needed to speak to you

Just put my energy out there

To see if it could flow with yours

Where This Goes

I'm ready to send that first text

The first step

To see if you was really feelin' me

I got your number yesterday

Have you been checking your phone constantly

Hoping that an unknown number would pop up

To continue the conversation we had when we met

I hope you didn't forget

How we smiled and shook hands

How it took courage for me to approach

I was a bit nervous

But still went through with getting to know you

I was afraid of getting rejected

But even more afraid of letting you go

Without knowing if we could have mended

Who Will I Be?

Don Juan De Marco?

The smooth like gigolo?

Swiping like Zorro?

Piping like Mario?

Or will I be the committed one?

The giving one?

The never splitting one?

The kissing one?

Under the distant sun?

Loyal to the Kingdom?

Mi Medicina

I can't wait to hear your voice

My pain reliever

My main believer

My ultimate motivator

My instant healer

My Spring Fling

There's only one lady out there

I would give it all away for

There's only one smile

I would give up my pay for

There's only one kiss

I would stay for

There's only one ear

I would play for

You're the only

You're the only one

Be There For You

I don't delve unless I'm certain

I won't make a mess in a garden

A beautiful atmosphere

Deserves a caretaker

Not a heartbreaker

Someone who's going tend to and not pretend to

Mend you when storms come

Send you nourishment with the sun

Everyday you deserve to feel ripe

Not just when disaster strikes

And when you're blossoming

When your leaves grow strong

I'll be there to celebrate how you germinate

Notification

How I wish I could just call you

Unleash all my emotions

How I wish I could just spoil you

Unleash all my devotions

Release all my anxieties

All my insecurities,

Would just cease to exist

When enveloped in your kiss

We could be beautiful together

We could be so special together

We would make the sweetest music

A soundtrack to love's deepest secrets

Showstopper

You're so amazing and breathtaking

What we could be making

Will never be forsaken

Or taken advantage of

Pure love is what we'd be striving for

Every morning rising for

The delight of having you in my life more

Photographic Memory

Is it flattering to feel the shattering

Knowing that you can make me vulnerable

So fragile to the insults you deliver

I wake up in a river of anxiety

I'm drowning in humiliation

I don't have the patience

To let my emotions pass

I hold on fast

I am slow to release

Focus on your every word

Remember everything I heard

I wish I could erase the bad files

And just remember the smiles

But I actually think more of the pain

Pumping poison in my veins

Mystified

Can't wait to see you

Yet I'm so nervous

Yet I'm so afraid

I still can't stay away

I'm so magnetized by your eyes

You're pulling me closer

You're taking over

Your magnetism has me in a trance

Every time I think of you

I feel so confused

Your beauty electrifies me

But also mystifies me

Cause I don't know if the vibe is mutual

Your words and actions are too ambiguous

Getting Anxious

When do you want to chill

Cause I can't sit still

I'm feeling impatient

It's mentally draining

Just waiting

For you to bless me with your presence

We need to set apart some time

Before my nerves rip apart my spine

Ready

I could probably speak to you forever

Words and emotions perfectly come together

You're the source of my happiness

It's kind of ridiculous

How one person could have this effect on me

How you could resurrect me

Every time I think of you

There's elation mixed with frustration

Cause I want you to be here physically

Even though the fantasy is so healing

So damn appealing

But who knows how much better

It will be when we're actually together

Unappreciated

I forgot what heartache felt like
The restless night
Slipping on ice
Missing someone you barely know
Wishing someone would repair the stones
A quake she left behind
A shaking that slows down the time
I'm barely maintaining
Heartbroken like a forgotten painting
Covered up in a dusty attic
A beautiful piece of art
That never got to hang on a living room wall
Or in a showcase
Or in a museum
Just forgotten

Trade With Me

Maybe if I give the homeless man on the train all my money

Maybe if I help every elderly person with their bags

The universe will pay me back

The universe will give me what I want

If I feed all the plants

Save all the animals

Tutor all the young ones

Never say no again to a friend

Will the universe give me her

Is that too much to ask for?

Is she too valuable?

Is it a fair trade?

Maybe the universe owes me this one

Thirsty

It's getting frustrated

An insane loneliness

I've been aching for this woman

I have the weakest grip on this situation

I wish I could just demand to spend some time

Go out for wine

Just watch a goddamn movie with me

But I can't come across too needy

Too desperate

Too creepy

Too threatening

Maybe I shouldn't have said anything

I should have stayed away

Because now that I got just a taste of her

I want to bathe with her

Just an ounce has me thirsting for the full amount

Still Fly

I'm an amazing person

I know this girl has me

But if she doesn't like me back

It's fine

I'm still a great guy

I'm good looking

I'm funny

I'm nice to everyone

That won't change

I just was hooked

And if she is throwing me off the hook

I have to go on and swim

I shouldn't feel like a failure

Just because one woman doesn't want me

There'll be others

There'll be more lovers

Bump On The Road

You don't know her situation

You have to show patience

Things don't always run smoothly

Sometimes there's a stop and go

A stutter to the flow

A hiccup

A slip up

A pause to the drip drop

A trip to the pitstop

A scratch on the wristwatch

Chillin'

I'll probably spend the afternoon

Daydreaming about you in that dress

Strolling through the bending roads of the park

Molding in the descending glow of the yellow

We never want the day to end

Cause we know the second

We dismiss each other

We're going to miss each other

Hey There

Hey there

I don't mean to stare

But I just can't look away

You got me in a daze

Hey there

I don't mean to stare

But your ambience

Has me in such a trance

Hey there

I don't mean to stare

But I need to formulate a conversation

I need to get your information

Slow

I haven't felt this way in so long

Writing words to a new love song

I feel like telling you everything

But I don't want to scare you away

I'd rather you stay another day

Stay in the realm of possibility

Fantasies are nice but they're a slippery slope

They're full of hope

But I can't reveal how I feel too early

Fearful of what you'd do if you heard me

Bliss

Just imagine a night of passion
Every second feels like Heaven
All our actions overlapping
Not a moment seems like less than a dream
In a whirlwind of a blessed vision
New discoveries answering the mysteries
Enhancing the trance of this eternal dance

Tus Ojos

Jewels glistening in the dim moonlight
Extending their attention in my direction
And sending electric currents
Not easy to handle such beauty
If I look away though I'll regret it
No other orbs can my heart absorb
Equivalent to a pink sunset in the distance

Rich

Just because I've never seen a shooting star
Even if I never drive a million dollar car
All those things wouldn't matter
Not even come close
If I could be the source of your laughter
Next to you today and the day after
Everyday running to you faster

The Night Before

Need a good night's sleep
Cause tomorrow I need the energy
Meeting her at Union Square
We're gonna see a movie there
Hopefully we'll click real quick

In My Arms

I don't know what the future holds
But I know what I want to hold
I want to hold your precious body
Just rest and close your eyes
I'm here to help heal
Wrap you in my arms of steel

The Beach

Let me feed you your favorite fruit

While you lay in your bathing suit

Feel the sun kissing our bodies

Smell the the sand within the breeze

Grab my hand and don't let go

As we watch the pace of the waves grow

Happy To See You

To what do I owe the honor
Seeing you feels like karma
Tell me why you've returned

Volcano

The more I learn about you

The more precious you become

The more I want to be part of your Queendom

The more time we spend

The more I can't pretend to hold it all in

I need to release every emotion

Every word is like an explosion

Just bursting

Showing how much I have been thirsting

Looking

I just want to sit so close

Look into each other's eyes

With no fear

No judgement

Seeing through

Not turning away

Just being amazed

By the intricate maze

In your translucent gaze

Traveling through fluorescent lanes

Taking me to a mystical paradise

Just from looking into your eyes

Crazy Busy

It's not that I'm not into you
I just got so much shit to do

I'll Be Waiting

If you're Ms Busy, Ms Independent

I'll be Mr Patient

I'll be at the other side of the bridge

You don't even have to move

I'll come to you

As soon as you give me the okay

I'll will be on my way

Personal Space

I'll let you breathe
You don't have to trip
Give you the space you need
I know you're busy
I know you work hard
I know you got a lot going on

Pumping

You might not know it yet

But I gonna make you soaking wet

You're gonna pull me inside

Holding on to the back of my arms

Moaning in my ear

Whispering your satisfaction

It's gonna be so indulging

Bodies pulsing

Time will slow down

But we'll be breathing so fast

Hearts pumping from the first to the last gasp

Fly With you

I don't care

I don't give a damn

I'm gonna be your man

I don't want to approach too aggressively

But I truly believe it's destiny

We're two angels that should be playing in the clouds

We don't deserve to be staying on the ground

Far And Near

We might be miles away

Where our smiles fade

But I've got a feeling

I'm still believing

We'll be connected

We're just being tested

I'm just so magnetized

To your soulful eyes

I want to slow dance with you

While I kiss you under the night's mist

I might miss a comet or a shooting star or two

But I don't want to miss you

My Knight

Shadows gliding through the alleys

Ghosts sliding through the trees

Terrible terrors terrorizing the lands

But there she stands

Golden chainmail and holding a glowing flail

Bashing all the demons back to hell

Summer 2016

Missing Her

Is she drifting away

Was she just a dream

A spring shower that dried up

Did I really know her

Did I really get to spend time

With a dime who was kind

Then left the line

It feels like she's so far

A distant fading star

A Good Day

I want to put my arms arounds you
And kiss the back of your neck
That's all I want to do
My day has been a train wreck
But if I get to hold you
It will still be a good day

Her Reward

She's busy, she focused

She's career driven, so ambitious

She travels the globe

She spreads her love

She gives so much to others

And I know she gets so much in return

Because everybody loves her back

But I want to give her something she's been missing

The thing she's been avoiding

Something so anointing

I want to give her that feeling

That ultimate high

That fortunate sky

Another Summer Tease

She's such a tease

She pulls you in

And then release

She gets you all hype

You think your the one she likes

You want to touch her body

But you're just a temporary hobby

So it's time to cut her off

Trust me you're better off

She's such a tease

She pulls you in

And then release

Keepin' My Cool

I was so nervous

When I asked you out that day

Not sure if you noticed

So afraid of what you'd say

The Second Date

My dream come true part two

Has arrived

On a hot rainy day that's gray

In July

The weather might mess things up

Or make things better

Depending on how clever

I can make this endeavor

I want to impress this woman

I want to make a testament

To why I'd be worth her investment

But in reality I shouldn't apply that pressure

An extra stressor

I should just be myself and have a good time

She's bound to come around

She's destined to be mine

Walking In Heaven

What can I say
You take my breath away
Blessed to spend the day
With an angel

Nothing I'd rather do
Then walk with you
Down Ninth Avenue

We laugh as we pass the grass
We relate by the lake
We learn more as we detour
We say our goodbyes as the rain dries

I take the long train ride home,
Mad that I'm alone
Wishing our date never ended
I go to bed with the memories of you in my head
Hoping when I awake, that it wasn't fake

Affection

I just want to make you laugh

So you can take my grasp

And spend a little time with me

Creating new memories

Relating to tendencies

Whatever stress you feel

Just let it blow away in the breeze

Let me hold your body please

I don't mean to beg you

But I can't settle for just thoughts

My Time With You

Freckles y besos

Jokes and deep thoughts provoked

A combination that sends sensations

To all sensitive and physical locations

Every moment with you

Is a token of truth

That takes me to ecstasy

That makes me view electricity

Use Me

Let me be your canvas

Let me be your blank page

Don't be afraid to illustrate

What frustrates

Whatever aggravates

What devastates

I might not be able to always elevate your state

But I'll always bring out your inner artist

Let you express and bring out your mess

As well as your best

Dealing With The Truth

I know I may never hear from you again

I can't pretend to be one of your priorities

If you don't show the same desire I pulse with

If this need isn't mutual

I must let it go

It's not fair to me

To not live so carefully

I want you to be with me

But not if it's so sparingly

Not Mutual

Maybe it's just not our time

Perhaps in another dimension

We are experiencing something totally different

We share an ecstasy only known to unearthly beings

A combination of euphoria and dreaming

But for now at this moment of time and space

We're distant and not on the same page

Time And Space

We'll eventually be

Can't you see it's destiny

You can't infinitely avoid me

Even when we cease to breathe

Even when this world implodes from it's core

My soul will seek out yours

This is an eternal longing

The minutes and hours of this existence are only the beginning

After Your Trip

I hope you return with something that you learned

I hope you arrive with hope in your eyes

I hope you realized that this is our time

That this is our chance to intertwine

We left things kind of up in the air

We left things kind of unclear

But now that your back

I hope we can chat

And decipher what we feel

Decide which way we're turning the wheel

Let's be truly honest then and confess then

What we truly want to address then

I want us to be straightforward

I want us both to be more heard

Just For An Instant

For a split second you smiled at me
In a way you never have before
For a split second you gazed at me
In a way that reached my shore
For a split second you changed to me
In a way that blurred all distraction
All I could see was sweet satisfaction
You feeling joy from my actions
The thought of possessing the ability to do that
Made me feel like the most powerful diplomat

What's The Deal, Damn It???

So, what's up girl?

You're back from the other side of the world

We got a couple more weeks of summer

Are you going to make me your lover?

Cause that really is the deadline

In the spring we did our thing

But you're still not mine

Our time is slipping away

If you just want to play

That's fine

Just tell me where you're coming from

Cause when I tell you how I feel

You always start to run

Fall 2016

Cause I Got You

I don't need to come home at 5am
I don't need to flirt with a friend
I don't need to run around this town
I don't need to find someone to revive the fun

Because you do it all
You're more than enough
You're always there when I call
You're more than enough
You give me love all night long
You're more than enough
You can do no wrong
Cause you're more than enough

Don't

Please don't take me for granted

Don't try to take advantage

You know I would spend my last dime

You know they'll never be a last time

I'll give you all the chances in the world

I'll give you all the romances in the world

You got me so damn hooked

All my days are booked

All I want to do is spend time with you

Walk down the street and kiss you

I don't ask for much and you know that

I simply blush from just being in contact

Your laugh makes me pat myself on the back

Your pretty face can erase the background of any space

And seem like we're the only ones in the place

So please don't take me for granted

Don't try to take advantage

Bumping Into You

I see you walking your Pomeranian on a Friday evening

I see you got that tight dress on

Making me want to press on

I think I'll ask you what your plans are

Cause you look so good from afar

Imagine what it must be like when I get close

I might freeze, even though I'll be sweating

I might get tongue tied, even though I want to talk to you all night

You look too good to let the moment slip

I'll probably rush my words

I'll probably stare at your curves

Either you'll think I'm pathetic

Or just a silly romantic

So Close

I almost had you

I almost made you mine

Others may say it was a waste of time

Why do I act so kind?

It's not a big deal to me

It was still real to me

We might have just dated for a bit

But hopefully you like what you tasted

And maybe it was too overwhelming

Too spicy, too rich, too thick of an icing

Perhaps later on, my dish will get reintroduced

And you'll find this distinct taste more delicious

Be Fearless

What is that you're so afraid of?

Was I talking too much about love?

Was I thinking too much ahead?

Should I have I talked about other things instead?

Should I have focused on just jokes and dancing?

Was I making too many advances?

See, I can't help who I am

And how I feel about women

I want to delve in your mind

I want to unwind your heart's bind

Disappointed

Its devastating the way you disappeared
This is what I feared
That you would leave me right at this point
It shrinks my insides how you disappoint
I had so many expectations for us
Just a few were actually discussed
But in my mind I had infinite plans

On My Mind

Its keeping me from sleeping

Can't do anything with meaning

My focus is only on one thing

My mind is traveling

When others are babbling

I'm weaving all kinds of intimate dreaming

Deep breathing and a woman screaming

Deep touching and blood rushing

Keep on pumping if she keeps on coming

Stimulating instrumentations of our lovemaking

Can We?

Can I meet you after work?

Can we go to the park?

I miss you

Even though we didn't chill much

I remember everything you said

Saved it in my memory bank

In my treasure box

And now I'm ready to break the lock

No Hard Feelings

I hope the best for you

I hope you get your skyline view

On Park Avenue

I hope you meet a man

With a good heart and strong hands

I hope you have a child

That has your witty smile

Excitement

I wish that one day out the blue

I'll get a text from you

I'll get so excited when I see your name

I'll feel so delighted you reignited the flame

Time hasn't made my feelings change

Maybe I stored my emotions away

But now they are bursting like a sun ray

The Combination

Come on now

You know my style is so unique

The perfect mix of a gentleman and a freak

A man in his peak

A man with experience, very equipped

Who's not afraid to learn new tricks

Fresh cut, Fresh kicks

Best strut, best lips

Waiting

Waiting for your response

Waiting for the fish to take the bait

Waiting for the butterfly to land on my finger

Aggressive

Sorry if I was a bit forward

But I was starting to get a bit impatient

A bit frustrated

I swear that this crush is authentic

I don't want to rush it

But I also don't want it to slip,

from a loose grip

I want to hold you as soon as possible

And as long as possible

Pressing your body in a passionate embrace

Testing your body in a practice race

Before we participate in a more intimate pace

I Like The Sound Of That

She's calling my name

Sometimes it's a muffled whisper

Sometimes it's a visceral yell

But every time it's special

Levitation

The more time we spend together
The more I soar in your comforting sky
I can always rely on your presence taking me high
Lifting me from the lowly earth…

Text back

On my train ride to work
Just crossed the Manhattan Bridge
Thinking about what I just did
I'll be waiting for her response anxiously
For the confirmation or the tragedy

Creativity

So many possibilities

So many potential surprises

Will be arising from our minds

And then be sculpted into existence

To be discovered by all the senses

When we paint a landscape

The passion we create

With every stroke

With every note

Reality expands to our demands

The universe will burst to the words of our chorus

Choreography altering astronomy

Our instruments make dents in planets

Prove To Me

You would take a bus
If you cared about us
You'd get on that plane
If you felt the same

But you say you're busy
And can't meet up with me

I miss you so deeply
I wish you came to see me
If you truly enjoy my comfort
Patience is a virtue
But I'd have more trust in you
If I saw more effort

Never Still

There's something about her soft features

That makes me want to keep her

But she likes to drift

She never sits

She always knows the closest exit

Take It Off

I'm so sorry for getting home late

I'm so sorry for making you wait

But don't pretend to be tired

I know you still feel the fire

You're trying to hold back your smile

You still want to be angry for a while

But do you mind undressing in the meantime

I promised once you rid of all your clothes

And I touch your bare skin

You'll start curling your toes and moaning

Inspires

She makes me feel like a sultan

She takes me higher than a mountain

She understands me to my core

Over sands and seas she makes me soar

Movement

Can you keep up

As it heats up

Body beat up

To the quick tempo

So simple

Just be nimble

Feels natural

Non-manual

Round 2?

Our affair might have been brief
I don't care, I still feel the grief
I miss you as if we were an eternal couple
Not hearing from you is such a struggle
And if you showed up out of the blue
I would definitely affectionately accept you
I don't mind that you gave me the cold shoulder
Because my cold days would be over

So if you want to reintroduce your truth
I'm down for something more absolute

F The Universe

It's just not fair

Stuck in our worlds

Too far from each other

Too much space and time

In between us

It makes me curse the universe

Should Have Been Happened

We could have been doing

What we're doing a long time ago

But we always seemed not to be single

At the exact time

We were always faithful to our lovers

We acted so cold to each other

We knew we had to protect

We showed true respect

So even now it's seems slow as hell

Still protecting the overflow of the well

Winter 2016/17

Residue

Why, oh why?

Am I

Still thinking about you

You ain't even that fly

But you still haunt my mind

Like a spirit still drifting

I think I'm slipping

Back into my coma

I know it's over

But I'm still caught up in the aroma of the aura

We only went out a few times

Who knew in due time

You blew my mind

Every date felt like a vacation

Drunk off every conversation

I put in so much work to impress you

But I never got to undress you

I barely even kissed you

But I still feel the residue

Overtime

I got so much going on
But girl you got me sprung
I live a hectic life
Can't predict the night
Anything can happen
I might come home late from work
My bad, don't be mad
Just give me next weekend
And I'll give you a place to sleep in
Trust me I'll be your everything
But today I'm working

The Plan

If you want to chill
Just let me know
If you need a drink
Then let's go
Baby I'm here for you
We don't have to leave until two
Finish the night off right
Let's kiss by the candle light
In the morning we can say goodbye
Then in a couple of days we can reunite

You Got Me

Did you forget how much I'm into you

Did you let your insecurities fool you

Don't you doubt how deep my loving goes

I'll take my time like winter snow

Caressing you with a flurry of tender kisses

Testing all your limits and inhibitions

I don't want you to slip from my grasp

That's why I laugh

When you act like that

Cause if you only knew

What I'm willing to do

Don't Take It Personal

I might have to kiss and say goodbye

This might seem like a big lie

But sorry I got to fly

Duty calls

And I must pick up

Not sure when you'll hear from me

No disrespect

So don't try to inspect

It's nothing personal

It's just business

Can't Touch You

Why would they hurt you

Maybe they were just too jealous

But you're here with me today

Mascara running down your face

Dress torn and stained

There's a scent of wine

You don't want to speak

You just want to stare into the trees

I touch your bare shoulder

And you don't seem to notice

You tightly shut your lips

I want to kiss

But I'm afraid you would just ignore me

Afraid you would abhor me

For blocking your view of the trees

Treasures

I can't escape your sexy seductive stare

Fichas shining through the *cortinas* of your hair

Telling me to come inside

Yelling for me to reside

In your intimate temple

To take the steps to your tight entrance

Touch the hidden switch

And say the secret pitch

Then enter deep within

Exploring all your rich possessions

Not ignoring a single item

All your treasures seduce me

All your valuables induce me

So spellbound by the beauty

Thinking And Listening

I'm aching, just taking so much time out of my day thinking about you

You're probably not even wasting any of your thoughts on me

And that should be enough to just let go

But it makes me want you more

I need to conquer your soul

I need to reach this goal

It's such a challenge

But still I manage

To think of ways to persuade you

To think of ways to sway you

I want to heal all your wounds

I want to hear all your tunes

Tell me everything you're embarrassed of

I swear not to judge, but only to love

I swear not to use your words against you

If I'm just given the chance to

Memories

I thought I was over you

But bumping into you the other day

Reminded me of how much I missed you

How much I want our story to continue

I don't want our memories to erode

I want to you see you again

I want to see where we can take this

If we can make this

Into something special

I miss strolling down the street and laughing

I miss rolling around the stream and asking

Questions that tell our tales

Your beauty breaks the scales

I can't get your face off my mind

Can I get a taste back into time?

2 AM

If this is just a dream

Then I don't want to wake up

Even if it's all made up

Because I don't think

I can take another break up

I just want stay up

In the middle of night

Seeing your body in the TV light

Guardian

I came to heal

My name is real

I'm not a figment of your imagination

I've got a filament of your destination

I've got your back through it all

I'll spot out the holes before you fall

I'll run to you when you call

It's not difficult for me to be there for you

I swear it's natural to take care of you

I'll fare very well in the lair of you

She's Not Playing Me

She's back in my system

She's back in my vision

But the truth is she never left

She's consumed me

Since she's made room for me

I bet she's pretty busy now

But she has time to play with my emotions

She can twist and bend me

Pretend to be more than a friend to me

But I don't mind

Cause I know the situation

It's a risk I'm willing to take

If my heart breaks

I don't give a damn

I knew that was part of the plan

If it doesn't work it's fine now

I'll move on quicker this time around

Do Over

We're spinning around once again
Will it turn into something
Or dissolve like the last time
I just miss our conversations
I just miss making you laugh
I just want another chance

Bad Timing

Are you sure this is what you want

I got you in my grasp

Will you be worth the hunt

You live so free

Do you have room for me

Don't be sorry

I prefer honesty

And if you can't see this working

I totally understand

I know you've got a lot of plans

I'm not going to hate on your career

You're getting closer every year

To the woman you want to become

And if that causes you to run

I won't hunt you down

Even though, I want you now

I'll live my life and so will you

And if we cross paths ever again

We can try things then

Picking Up The Pace

Sorry, I took so long

But me, I take my time

I ease so I can please

Then let it all rush in

Even when I'm crushing

I'm a slow brook sometimes overlooked

Once I get into the flow of things

I'm a wild river bashing and crashing

Secrecy

So you're leaving

Following what you've been dreaming

But what about my dreams to be with you

I've never said how I've been feeling

But before you go, maybe I should let it out

Get it out my system

Show you my visions

Would it change your decision?

Just One Night

Give me just one night

To excite my taste buds

Just give me the right

To taste your love

I need to have you

Even if it's just for a moment

I'll be so focused

On making you climax

I won't bypass

Any stops

I'll kiss every single spot

Just give me a shot

I'm sure to deliver

Make you come in the clutch

Hit the game winner

Make you moan so much

I'll be so relentless in your body

I'll be so invested in your body

I'd Be Free In Your Freedom

I wish you were free

So I can run wild by your side

And I didn't have to hide

My emotions for you

My devotion for you

It would be so extreme

But it's just a dream

I can't intervene

I have to let you be

But if you were free

I'd embrace you deeply

So you can really see me

Broke Feelings

Maybe if I had more funds

Maybe if I wasn't scraping for crumbs

She'd be with me already

But instead she's…

Messed Up

Last time we spoke

You seemed to be interested

Now it's more of a joke

You don't seem invested

Why do you play these games?

I know you like attention

But it's wrong to distinguish flames

And leave me in the dark guessing

Baby I'm Gone

We started off so explosive
But the smoke has settled
I ran out of feelings to give
There's no reaching the next level
I apologize for leading you on
Sorry Baby, I'm gone

I know I said you were my muse
The only one I would choose
And when I said it, I meant it
Please believe me, I never lied to you
But if I remained now
I'd be hiding the truth
Because I'm ready to move on
Sorry, Baby but I'm gone

You can call me an asshole

You can call me a jerk

I didn't back up what I told

I left you full of hurt

I'm obviously the bad guy

There's no reason to lie

I'm not going to put a sugar coat on

Sorry, Baby but I'm gone

Remember Me

Winter is almost over

The days won't be getting colder

The leaves will return

The sun again will start to burn

The city will be calling your name

Just don't forget me, darling

I hope you remember last spring

A Wolf's Message

Running in the darkness of the forest

Padded paws hitting the dirt and grass

Hopping over logs and whispering rivers

Just to get to the hill to see that globe of silver

Sending you a message with my heart pounding and howling

Confusion

Push and pull
Tear and rebuild
Not sure why you do this
Why you seem to dismiss
When were about to kiss
You take your leave
Right when I can't breathe
Your timing is a disgrace
To my empty embrace

Right Here

You live so close
But I never see you
If you ever feel lost
You know what to do
I'll be here waiting
I've been aching
So when you finally come
I'll be fully healed

Spring 2017

A Close Friend

I know you're going through a lot

Life seems like a mess

But give me a shot

To restore some happiness

Making you laugh makes me whole

I think about you all day long

Your presence turns my elements to gold

Romantic visions while listening to a love song

I'm happy to have known you

But I wish it was more

I need to hold you

I want the passion to pour

Stop Playin' With Me

You drew me back in

Maybe just for attention

Maybe to cause confusion

You might like the chaos

The battle of emotional violence

But that's just not me

I rather be completely happy

Than to be taken to a beach of quicksand

Don't fool me with the sun and the breeze

I don't want to sink and suffocate

I want to breathe and levitate

A friendship that ascends to the ends of the universe

I want to progress and live with purpose

Romance By The Sea

Meet me at corner of Surf and Stillwell

Greet me with a kiss in the mist

Of the sea salt smell

Smile and talk as we approach the boardwalk

Whispers turn to loud laughs

Gentle touches turn to sensual grasps

Intoxicated from the pheromones

Living dreams that seemed unknown

They'll never be another like this

The reason why we exist

Passionate words and embraces

Smiling and understanding faces

Every syllable is heard

Every emotion is seen

Senses enhanced by the lustful gleam

Trying To Forget

Wish I could lock it all way

Throw away the key today

And never ever open up those memories

I just want to live in the present realities

But a part of me still believes

Those days can somehow be retrieved

Why do they mean so much to me

Even if they were incomplete

Just moments of talking in the street

Sweating in the summer heat

Increasing my heartbeat

Every time we meet

Ingesting the words you speak

Let Me Know

Tell me what I gotta be

Do you want a stronger man

Do I have to lift weights

Do you want a richer man

Do I have to buy real estate

Tell me what I gotta be

To make you my baby

I'll become everything you desire

I'll keep reaching higher

I'll be more ambitious and luxurious

If it will make you more curious

Tell me please

Wake Up

One of these days you'll realize who I am

It'll hit you like a ton of bricks

I should be more than just a friend

And all this back and forth was ridiculous

Do Your Thing

You don't have to feel guilty
If you haven't been totally honest with me
We were just chillin', having a good time
You do your thing
And I'll do mine

See you're not tied down
So you can go check around
Cause we just chillin, having a good time
You do your thing
And I'll do mine

Now don't hate me
If I chill with another lady
Don't get all pissed off and ticked off
Cause I know you got friends too
And this is what we agreed to do

City Of Goddesses

If you want to see true beauty

All you gotta do is come to my city

So much variety

That it's an oddity

Everywhere you go, they're around

Uptown or downtown

East or West

A queen and a goddess

Don't expect any less

Testing Different Waters

I just might be afraid

To give it all away

I just want to give some here

And some over there

To see where I want to go

And with who I want to share

Two Of A Kind

I don't do these type of events often
So it's easy for me to get lost in
Once I see someone familiar
A smiling face by the window
She saves me from this bouginess
She's the one with real classiness

Frustration Building

Staying up in the middle of the night

Waiting for you to hit me up

It just ain't right

You know what you are doing to me

I'm trying to play it off smoothly

But it's frustrating waiting for a response

Why are you hesitating so much

I don't want to make a fuss

But I'm getting pissed off

Options

If I come back will you open the door

See I had to travel the world

I never was dishonest, never broke a promise

But in the middle of it all you revealed

That you might not be able to handle my steel

I want to see who else can wield and hold the shield

Your beauty and sex appeal could kill

But I want to know if another can peel my heart's seal

Break Time

I need some extra strength

To be by myself

Take some days to lay

And just contemplate

If you're worth the wait

Or even if it's too late

Or did it even permeate

Maybe I'll never break

Through your defenses

In case this is senseless

And I need to drift off into the distance

And I need to submit into a new existence

Having nights that don't consist of your potential kiss

I have to let this dream deteriorate

Before it makes my life beam deteriorate

www.ingramcontent.com/pod-product-compliance
Lightning Source LLC
Chambersburg PA
CBHW071204070526
44584CB00019B/2917